I SEE 1, 2, 3

Count Your Community with Sesame Street

Jennifer Boothroyd

Lerner Publications ◆ Minneapolis

Lerner Publications Company
An imprint of Lerner Publishing Group, Inc.
241 First Avenue North
Minneapolis, MN 55401 USA

For reading levels and more information, look up this title at www.lernerbooks.com.

Main body text set in Mikado Regular
Typeface provided by HVD Fonts.

Library of Congress Cataloging-in-Publication Data

Names: Boothroyd, Jennifer, 1972- author.
Title: I see 1, 2, 3 : count your community with Sesame Street / Jennifer Boothroyd.
Other titles: I see one, two, three | Sesame Street (Television program)
Description: Minneapolis : Lerner Publications, [2020] | Audience: Ages 4-8. |
    Audience: K to grade 3. | Includes bibliographical references.
Identifiers: LCCN 2019014603 (print) | LCCN 2019019823
    (ebook) | ISBN 9781541583337 (eb pdf) | ISBN 9781541572638 (lb : alk. paper) |
    ISBN 9781541589254 (pb : alk. paper)
Subjects: LCSH: Counting—Juvenile literature. | Arithmetic—Juvenile literature. |
    Muppets (Fictitious characters)—Juvenile literature.
Classification: LCC QA113 (ebook) | LCC QA113 .B6425 2020 (print) | DDC 513.2—dc23

LC record available at https://lccn.loc.gov/2019014603

Manufactured in the United States of America
1-46530-47575-8/27/2019

Sesame Street has always been a trusted partner when it comes to building math skills in young children, helping them learn to problem-solve, and preparing them for school. Count on the familiar furry friends of *Sesame Street* to make it fun, by finding math moments in the everyday. Ready?

1, 2, 3, go!

Greetings, everybody! It is I, Count von Count! I am counting my books. *Ah, ah, ah!* Counting is a wonderful way to explore. Let's take a counting journey in your community. *Ah, ah, ah.*

1 one book

2 two books

3 three books

Tall buildings have many floors. The elevator counts the floors as it moves up.

Floor 1, 2, 3, 4.

That's a Fact! The Empire State Building in New York is 102 floors high.

Look around your room at home.
You can count your favorite things.

I like counting my paper clips. I see 1, 2, 3 . . .

Counting keeps us safe at the crosswalk. A timer starts with big numbers and counts down. It counts backward. Only 8, 7, 6, 5 seconds left.

That's a Fact! Many crosswalk signals make sounds to help people who have trouble seeing.

Remember to hold a grown-up's hand while you cross a street.

The grocery store is full of things to count.

You pick up 4 apples.

Then you choose 6 bananas.

That's 10 pieces of fruit all together.

What other things can you count at the grocery store?

Count while coloring. The green group of crayons is bigger than the purple group.

There are MORE green crayons.

There are FEWER purple crayons.

Elmo uses lots of colors in Elmo's drawings. How many different colors do you count?

That's a Fact! The biggest crayon-making company makes **12 million** crayons a day.

What can you count while you're on the go?

Bike wheels zoom by.

I see **2, 4, 6** wheels in a line.

What else can you count by twos?

There are 2 people and 2 wheels on a tandem bike.

Kids kick their feet in the pool.

Each foot has 5 toes.

There are 5, 10, 15, 20, 25, 30 toes.

That's a lot of toes!

I like to play with toys in the water. How many toys can you see?

That's a Fact! A swimming pool for the Olympics is **164** feet (50 m) long.

It is exciting to go to the bowling alley.

There are 10 pins in each lane.

You can count the pins by tens.

Count **10, 20, 30, 40, 50, 60** pins.

Bowling pins can crash so loudly! I love it!

Hang up your coat when you come inside.

First, there are 3 coats hanging up.

Then 1 more coat is added.

How many coats are there now?

I, Super Grover, always hang up my cape when I have finished saving the day.

That's a Fact! The coldest place on Earth where people live is in Russia. You would need a coat to keep you warm there in the -76°F (-60°C) temperatures.

The library is full of things to count.

There are 7 library books on a shelf.

You check out 1 book.

How many books are left?

I like to read books and look at the pictures. And I can count the pages in the books too.

The playground is busy.

The **FIRST** kid has a red shirt.

The **SECOND** kid has a shirt with stripes.

What color shirt is the **THIRD** kid wearing?

I hope you have enjoyed our counting journey, *ah, ah, ah*. What will you count next?

That's a Fact! Most playground slides are **24** inches across. That's **2** feet, or **61** cm!

Count the Slimeys!

This is Oscar's pet worm, Slimey. He's been visiting the pages of this book. Go back and count all the Slimeys you find.

Count the Ways

Look at the ways to show 4 with your fingers.

Now it's your turn. How many ways can you show 5?

Glossary

bowling: a game played by rolling a ball to knock down ten pins in a lane

community: a group of people that live, work, and learn in nearby places

crosswalk: a path marked for people to cross a street

elevator: a machine used for carrying people to different floors in a building

Olympics: games and sporting events held in different countries during the summer and winter once every four years

tandem: a group of two, such as two seats on a tandem bicycle

Further Information

Big Book of ABCs and 123s. Philadelphia: Running Press Kids, 2018.

Levit, Joe. *Let's Explore Math*. Minneapolis: Lerner Publications, 2019.

Marino Walters, Jennifer. *Numbers in Nature*. Egremont, MA: Red Chair, 2019.

PBS Kids: 123 Games
https://pbskids.org/games/123/

Sesame Street: Egg Counting Elmo
https://www.sesamestreet.org/games?id=25578

Topmarks: Underwater Counting
https://www.topmarks.co.uk/learning-to-count/underwater-counting

Index

Photo Acknowledgments

Additional image credits: Cunaplus_M.Faba/iStock/Getty Images, p. 5 (all); joreks/Shutterstock.com, p. 6; twobee/Shutterstock.com, p. 7; Katarzyna Bialasiewicz/iStockphoto/Getty Images, p. 8; EHStockphoto/Shutterstock.com, p. 9; rSnapshotPhotos/Shutterstock.com, p. 10; ballyscanlon/Photographer's Choice RF/Getty Images, p. 11; Kyselova Inna/Shutterstock.com, p. 12 (apple); bergamont/Shutterstock.com, p. 12 (Banana); B Brown/Shutterstock.com, p. 13; George Filyagin/Shutterstock.com, p. 14; Joanna Dorota/Shutterstock.com, p. 15; Hero Images/Getty Images, p. 16; Karl Weatherly/Getty Images, p. 17; JGI/Jamie Grill/Tetra Images RF/Getty Images, p. 18; Evlakhov Valeriy/Shutterstock.com, p. 19 (Beach Ball); JReizabal/Shutterstock.com, p. 19 (turtle); Jiri Vaclavek/Shutterstock.com, p. 19; Pilotsevas/Shutterstock.com, p. 19; Pavel V Mukhin/Shutterstock.com, p. 19; Ingram Publishing/Getty Images, p. 20; Lotus_studio/Shutterstock.com, p. 21; OZaiachin/Shutterstock.com, p. 22 (yellow jacket); Samuel Borges Photography/Shutterstock.com, p. 22; Karkas/Shutterstock.com, p. 22 (orange jacket, purple jacket); AndrewHeffernan/Shutterstock.com, p. 23; Independent Picture Service, p. 24; PeopleImages/Getty Images, p. 25; Jane September/Shutterstock.com, p. 26; gpointstudio/iStockphoto/Getty Images, p. 27; Lim Yong Hian/Shutterstock.com, p. 29 (hands).